MW00416844

Kenneth E. Hagin

Second Edition
Seventh Printing 1995

ISBN 0-89276-040-0

In the U.S. write:
Kenneth Hagin Ministries
P.O. Box 50126
Tulsa, Oklahoma 74150-0126

In Canada write:
Kenneth Hagin Ministries
Box 335, Station D,
Etobicoke, Ontario, M9A 4X3

Cover photo by Elwood Chess

Preface

Feed your faith daily! It is of utmost importance to your walk with the Lord. I've written these bite-size pieces of "faith food" to aid you in making sure your faith is fed daily.

F. F. Bosworth said, "Most Christians feed their bodies three hot meals a day, their spirits one cold snack a week, and then they wonder why they are so weak in faith."

Say the confessions found on the bottom of each page aloud. Close your eyes and repeat them. They are based on God's Word. When you hear yourself say these confessions, they will register on your spirit. And when God's Word gets down into your spirit, it will control your life!

Kenneth E. Hagin

Kenneth E. Hagin

Mark 11:23 and 24 keynote Kenneth E. Hagin's life and ministry.

He first believed these startling statements from the lips of Jesus while lying almost totally paralyzed and completely bedfast from a deformed heart and incurable blood disease. Doctors did not expect him to reach his 17th birthday.

But, after 16 months bedfast, he *believed* that those Scriptures mean what they say, *acted* upon them in simple faith, and rose up healed.

Later the Lord called him to *"Go teach my people faith."* In 1984, Rev. Hagin celebrated the 50th anniversary of this calling to emphasize the integrity of God's Word.

Alive

For the word of God is quick, and powerful, and sharper than any twoedged sword, piercing even to the dividing asunder of soul and spirit, and of the joints and marrow, and is a discerner of the thoughts and intents of the heart.
— HEBREWS 4:12

To be strong in faith, the first thing you must settle on is the integrity of the Word of God.

You must know that the Bible is exactly what it declares itself to be — God's Word — a revelation from God to us! It is God speaking to us now! It is not only a book of the past and the future; it is a book for now. It is a God-breathed, God-indwelt, God-inspired message.

Moffatt's translation of Hebrews 4:12 reads, "For the Logos [Word] of God is a living thing. . . ." Quick! Alive! Living! But it will come alive to you only as you accept it and act upon it.

I've always maintained the following attitude toward the Word of God, and have acted upon it accordingly: *The Word is just as though the Lord Jesus Christ were here in person speaking to me.*

Confession: *God's Word is alive. It is alive in me. God speaks to me through His Word. He gives me revelation through His Word. I accept His Word as though the Lord Jesus Christ Himself were here in person speaking to me. And I act upon it accordingly.*

Settled

For what if some did not believe? shall their unbelief make the faith of God without effect? God forbid: yea, let God be true, but every man a liar....

— ROMANS 3:3,4

To establish a firm foundation for your faith, I suggest you adopt the following motto which I wrote in red ink in the flyleaf of my Bible many years ago:

> The Bible says it.
> I believe it.
> And that settles it.

Determine to always do these two things: (1) Accept God's Word for what it says, and (2) Walk in the light of what the Word says. Don't try to get around certain things or explain them away. Don't try to read things into the Word just because you want to believe those things that way. Study the Word — and accept it just as it is written.

For example, the denomination I was reared in didn't teach faith and healing. I was bedfast sixteen months as a teenager, and five doctors said I had to die. But I turned to the Word of God, and the more I studied, the more I saw that the Word is true. I declared, "I am going to walk in the light of what the Word says, regardless of church teaching, because the Word of God is God speaking to me today." When I settled that issue in my mind, 60 percent of the battle was won: I was on the road to divine healing.

Confession: *God's Word is true. I believe God. I walk in the light of what the Word says, because the Word of God is God speaking to me today.*

Performance

Then said Jehovah . . . I watch over my word to perform it.
— JEREMIAH 1:12 ASV

In all probability, you have faith in your employer. You believe what he says, and you act on it. If he promises to raise your salary, you don't question him.

Also, you and your word are one. You are back of your word and your promises. If your word is no good, then you are no good.

But God's Word is more reliable than the word of a man! God's Word and God are one. If God's Word is no good and it cannot be relied upon, then God is no good, and He cannot be relied upon.

But He can be relied upon! He stands behind His Word! He stands behind every Word He promises!

You come to know Jesus through the Word of God. Jesus introduces you to God the Father. Then you begin to act upon God's Word. You test it. After a time of acting upon what God says in His Word, it becomes as natural to you as acting upon the word of the man for whom you are working.

Confession: *I believe God. I act upon His Word. Then He watches over His Word to perform it in my life.*

The Word

So then faith cometh by hearing, and hearing by the word of God. — ROMANS 10:17

"I just don't have any faith," some Christians say. "I've prayed and fasted for faith, but I just don't have any."

Asking for faith will never produce faith. Why not? Because faith doesn't come by *asking;* faith comes by *hearing.* By hearing what? The Word of God!

Having to encourage Christians to have faith means that the Word of God has lost its reality in their lives. None of the New Testament Epistles encourage believers to have faith. Why not? Because the Epistles were written to the Church. And its individual members are actually born into the family of God. Believers have received the Holy Spirit as their Teacher, Guide, and Comforter. And the measure of their faith will be the measure of their knowledge of their Father — and their knowledge of their privileges.

And that will be the measure of your faith too. Simply study the Bible and get acquainted with your heavenly Father. Walk in the closest possible fellowship with Him. Become familiar with your privileges as His child.

As you become one with the Word, and the Word becomes one with you, you will become mighty in faith.

Confession: *As I study the Word of God, I am becoming one with it. I am feeding upon it; I am hearing it; and faith is coming to me.*

The Witness

If we receive the witness of men, the witness of God is greater.... And this is the record, that God hath given to us eternal life, and this life is in his Son. He that hath the Son hath life....

— 1 JOHN 5:9,11,12

Faith will say about itself everything the Word says, because *faith in God is simply faith in His Word.*

Study God's Word with this determination: *I will find out what God says and agree with it.* You can't expect the things of God to work for you if you take sides *against* His Word. This may mean unlearning certain "religious" ideas. Too often we've been religiously brainwashed instead of scripturally taught.

Find out what God says in His Word regarding: (1) What God has wrought for us in His plan of redemption; (2) What the Father is to you; (3) What Jesus is doing for you now at the right hand of the Father; and (4) What the Holy Spirit is doing in you.

Then find out from His Word what God thinks about the following: (1) *What* He says you are in Christ; (2) *Who* you are in Christ; (3) What you *have* because you're in Christ.

Even though it may not seem real in your life, start confessing, "Yes, that's mine, according to God's Word." You will then find that faith's confession creates reality.

Confession: *I agree with the witness of God. What He says I am, I am. What He says I have, I have.*

5

Redeemed

In whom [Jesus Christ] *we have redemption through his blood. . . .* — EPHESIANS 1:7

Webster defines the word "redeem" as: (1) "To buy back"; (2) "To free from captivity by payment of ransom."

To walk in the highest kind of faith, you must know the reality of your redemption in Christ not as a doctrine, a philosophy, or a creed, but as an actual redemption out of the authority of Satan.

When Adam fell, mankind went into captivity.

But God had a plan — a great plan of redemption! And He sent the Lord Jesus Christ to consummate it. (Webster defines "consummate" as "complete in every detail: perfect.")

Now God's Word tells us *"In whom* [Jesus Christ] *we have redemption. . . ."* How thankful we can be that we're not trying to get redeemed. We already *have* redemption! We are redeemed and delivered *now* from the authority of darkness; from the power of Satan!

Confession: *I am redeemed! In Christ I have redemption! Through His blood I have redemption! I'm not trying to get it; it's mine. I have it now! Jesus bought me back. Jesus freed me from captivity by the payment of a ransom — His own life!*

Translated

Giving thanks unto the Father, which hath made us meet [able] *to be partakers of the inheritance of the saints in light: Who hath delivered us from the power* [authority] *of darkness, and hath translated us into the kingdom of his dear Son: In whom we have redemption through his blood. . . .*

— COLOSSIANS 1:12-14

Darkness is the kingdom of Satan. And in that word "darkness" is everything Satan is.

Light is the kingdom of God.

By means of the New Birth, you were translated out of the kingdom of darkness — and into the kingdom of God's dear Son, the kingdom of God, and the kingdom of light.

Our heavenly Father has fitted His children (or made them "meet") to partake of an inheritance — "the inheritance of the saints *in light*"! Part of your inheritance is that God has delivered you out of Satan's authority of darkness, and He has now translated you into the kingdom of His dear Son!

God *has* made you meet . . . He *has* delivered you . . . He *has* translated you. Thank God, you can partake of your inheritance *now*. Don't relegate it to the future.

Confession: *Thank You, Father. You have made me able to partake of my inheritance now. I am redeemed. I am delivered from the authority of Satan now. I am translated into the kingdom of your dear Son now. I am a citizen of the kingdom of light. I live in the light. I walk in the light. I am a saint in the light!*

Overcomer

*And they overcame him by the blood of the Lamb, and by
the word of their testimony....*

— REVELATION 12:11

Because Satan is the god of this world (2 Cor.
4:4), he will try to exercise authority over you in
this life. He will try to dominate you. He will try
to keep you from walking in your redemptive
rights.

But you can overcome the devil every time, no
matter where you meet him, and no matter what
the test. You can overcome him because of the
blood of the Lamb, and because of the word of your
testimony!

You simply have to know what the blood has
bought for you: deliverance from the power
(authority) of darkness (Satan) and translation (by
virtue of the New Birth) into the kingdom of light.
Then you have to add your testimony to that
knowledge.

Stand your ground. Confess what the blood of
the Lamb has wrought. Thank God, there is power
in the blood! But the power in the blood won't just
work automatically — you have to add your
testimony to it.

Confession: *I am an overcomer. I overcome the devil in
every confrontation; he never overcomes me. I overcome
him by the blood of the Lamb, and by the word of my
testimony.*

Dominion

. . . he [God] *raised him* [Christ] *from the dead, and set him at his own right hand in the heavenly places, Far above all principality, and power, and might, and dominion, and every name that is named, not only in this world, but also in that which is to come: And hath put all things under his feet, and gave him to be the head over all things to the church, Which is his body, the fulness of him that filleth all in all.*

— EPHESIANS 1:20-23

Once we are new creatures in Christ Jesus, Satan's dominion over us ended. Jesus is the Lord and Head of this new Body — the Church.

We are the Body. Christ is the Head. The Church is the Body. Christ is the Head.

The whole Body of believers — all the born-again ones — are new creatures in Christ Jesus. Then each of us individually is a new creature, too, because all of us are members of that Body.

Satan has no right to rule over the Body of Christ — and he has no right to rule over us individually either.

Christ is the Head of the Body. He is the One who is to rule and dominate the Body of Christ. Satan has lost his dominion over our spirits, our bodies, our minds, our finances, and the circumstances of our lives, because God has put *all things* under Christ's feet.

Confession: *God has put all things under Christ's feet. I am a member of the Body of Christ. The feet are in the Body, so Satan is under my feet!*

Custodian

What? know ye not that your body is the temple of the Holy Ghost which is in you, which ye have of God, and ye are not your own? For ye are bought with a price: therefore glorify God in your body, and in your spirit, which are God's.
— 1 CORINTHIANS 6:19,20

"Brother Hagin, our spirits belong to the Lord all right, but our bodies haven't been redeemed yet. So we have to go on suffering sickness and disease in the physical realm," some have said.

But in the text above, God's Word tells us that not only your spirit, but your body as well, is bought with a price. Therefore, we are told, "glorify God in your body. . . ."

Does God get glory out of the devil dominating us physically? Does God get glory when the temple of the Holy Spirit is being defaced with disease? No, certainly not.

Why does God permit it, then? Because *you* are the custodian of your body, the temple of God's Spirit. God said for *you* to do something about your body.

Learn to take a stand against anything that attacks your body just as quickly as you stand against whatever attacks your spirit. Simply say, "Satan, you don't have any right to put that on my body. My body belongs to God."

Confession: *My body is the temple of God. I will be a good custodian. I will glorify God in my body.*

Purchased

Do you not know that your body is the temple — the very sanctuary — of the Holy Spirit Who lives within you, Whom you have received [as a Gift] from God? You are not your own, You were bought for a price — purchased with a preciousness and paid for, made His own. So then, honor God and bring glory to Him in your body.

— 1 CORINTHIANS 6:19,20 *Amplified*

I like the way I saw a missionary, who had returned from the field, minister to the sick.

Ministering to one woman, he prayed first: "Father, this woman is your child. She belongs to You. It's not right for the devil to dominate her. You laid her sickness and disease on Jesus, for it is written, '... *Himself took our infirmities, and bare our sicknesses*'" (Matt. 8:17).

Then the missionary talked to the devil: "Satan, this woman's body is a temple of the Holy Ghost. It belongs to God, and you have no right to trespass on God's property. Remove yourself from God's property!"

Then he talked to the woman: "Satan has oppressed your body with sickness, but God has made provision for your deliverance. Your body is a temple of the Holy Ghost, and you are commanded to glorify God in your body. Can God be glorified in your body by the devil dominating it? No. Therefore, stand against this sickness with me. We *demand* that Satan stop trespassing on God's property!"

Confession: *I will honor God and bring glory to Him in my body.*

No Trespassing!

Leave no [such] room or foothold for the devil — give no opportunity to him.

— EPHESIANS 4:27 *Amplified*

I remember reading years ago in *Reader's Digest* about a lovely little patch of grass that people were prone to cut across. So the gardener built a small fence around this beautiful square of grass — just some small stakes and string. But people persisted in stepping over the string and walking across the grass. So the gardener painted a crude sign:

> Gentlemen *will not,*
> and others *must not,*
> trespass on this property!

That gave me the idea of putting up a sign on my body. You can't see it, because it's in the spirit. But the devil can see it. My sign says:

> NO TRESPASSING!
> DEVIL, THIS MEANS YOU!

I did that by faith. I've had that sign up for years now, and the devil doesn't trespass on God's property, my body.

As the custodian of your body, it's really your job to see to it that Satan does not trespass on God's property.

Confession: *As a custodian of God's property, I do not allow trespassers. I leave no room, nor do I even give a foothold for the devil. I allow him no opportunity.*

New Creation

Therefore if any man be in Christ, he is a new creature [creation]: *old things are passed away; behold, all things are become new.* — 2 CORINTHIANS 5:17

I'm glad I'm a new creature. I was only 15 when I was born again, but I remember exactly what happened. Something took place inside of me. It seemed as if a two-ton load rolled off my chest. Not only did something depart *from* me — but something came *into* me!

The moment you accepted Jesus Christ as your Savior and confessed Him as your Lord (Rom. 10:9,10), you, too, were recreated. At that moment, the redemption which Jesus provided 2,000 years ago became a reality to you. At that instant, the very life and nature of God were imparted to your spirit. You were recreated — born again!

The New Birth is not an experience. It is not a religion. It is not joining a church. *It is the actual birth of your spirit.*

When you were born again, old things passed away. In the sight of God, all sin and all of your past life were blotted out. All you had been — spiritually speaking — was blotted out. It ceased to exist. And you became a new man in Christ Jesus. God sees nothing in your life before the moment you were born again!

All things inside you became new. Your spirit was recreated. You passed from death unto life (1 John 3:14)!

Confession: *I am a new creature in Christ. I am a new creation. I am recreated. The life and nature of God are within me. I have passed from death unto life! I am a new creature!*

Family

But as many as received him, to them gave he power to become the sons of God, even to them that believe on his name: Which were born, not of blood, nor of the will of the flesh, nor of the will of man, but of God.

— JOHN 1:12,13

No truth in all the Bible is as far reaching as the blessed fact that when we are born again we come into the family of God! God the Father is our Father!

He cares for us! He is interested in us — each of us individually — not just as a group, or a body, or a church. He is interested in each of His children, and He loves each of us with the same love.

However, our heavenly Father is not the Father of everyone, as some suppose. Jesus said to some very religious people, *"Ye are of your father the devil ..."* (John 8:44). Yes, God is the Creator of all mankind, but a man must be born again to become His child. He is *God* to the world, but *Father* only to the new creation man.

God is your very own Father. You are His very own child. And since He is your Father, you can be assured that He will take a father's place and perform a father's part. You can be certain that as your heavenly Father, God loves you, and He will take care of you.

Confession: *I am born of God. I am born into God's family. God the Father is my Father. I am His very own child. He is my very own Father. He loves me. He provides for me. He takes care of me.*

Loved

I [Jesus] *in them* [believers], *and thou* [God the Father] *in me, that they may be made perfect in one; and that the world may know that thou hast sent me, and hast loved them, as thou hast loved me.*

— JOHN 17:23

When you know — really know — that God is your very own Father and you are His very own child, this knowledge will have the following effect on you: *You will have as much freedom and fellowship with the Father as Jesus had in His earth walk,* because God the Father loves you even as He loved Jesus! John 17:23 says so: *". . . and hast loved them, as thou hast loved me."*

"I just can't believe that God loves me as much as He loved Jesus," some may say.

Thank God, I can. I believe it, because the Bible says it, and that settles it!

You and I can say with Jesus, *". . . I am not alone, because the Father is with me"* (John 16:32). Because if God loves me as He loved Jesus — and He does — then He is with me as He was with Jesus. I am never afraid, just as Jesus was never afraid. There is nothing to fear. What can man do to the man or woman whom God loves and protects?

Confession: *God the Father is my very own Father. I am His very own child. And He loves me in my earth walk just as much as He loved Jesus in His earth walk. I can fellowship with Him just as Jesus did. I am free from fear just as Jesus was, for I am not alone. My Father is with me.*

Born Again

Being born again, not of corruptible seed, but of incorruptible, by the Word of God, which liveth and abideth for ever.
— 1 PETER 1:23

We are begotten of God.
We are born of God.
We are children of God.
We are heirs of God.
We are joint-heirs ("joint" means equal) with Jesus (Rom. 8:17).

In declaring this, we do not magnify ourselves. We magnify God and what He has done for us through the Lord Jesus Christ. We do not make ourselves new creatures. God made us new creatures. He is the Author and Finisher of our faith.

We are new creatures created by God in Christ Jesus!

Confession: *I am begotten of God. I am born of God. I am born of incorruptible seed by the living Word of God. I was born into the spiritual realm, given eternal life, and made a branch of the vine through the incorruptible Word of God.*

His Workmanship

For we are his workmanship, created in Christ Jesus unto good works, which God hath before ordained that we should walk in them.

— EPHESIANS 2:10

We believers didn't make ourselves who and what we are — God did. So be careful about passing judgment on God's creation.

Christians who think they are being humble, sometimes say, "I'm so unworthy." But God didn't make any unworthy new creations. I'm not unworthy, and you're not unworthy either. To say that you are unworthy is not humility — it is ignorance of the Word of God, and it gives place to the devil to dominate you.

We are God's workmanship! When you belittle yourself, you are actually complaining about what God has done. You're belittling His workmanship.

"Created in Christ Jesus," our Scripture says. Quit looking at yourself from the natural standpoint. Look at yourself *in Jesus*. You'll look much better. You see, God the Father doesn't see you like anybody else sees you. He sees you *in Christ!*

Confession: *I am God's workmanship. He made me a new creation. He created me in Christ Jesus. I see myself as God sees me. I see myself in Christ.*

Blotted Out

I, even I, am he that blotteth out thy transgressions for mine own sake, and will not remember thy sins.

— ISAIAH 43:25

"I guess I'm just paying for the life I lived before I got saved," a minister who was having a hard time once said to me.

Many Christians, like that minister, are defeated, permitting things to take place in their lives, because they think that's the way it has to be. They don't know the difference between *repentance* and *doing penance*. They try to do penance for their past life. But in reality, since they repented of their sins, God has no knowledge that they've ever done anything wrong!

"I blotted out your transgressions," God said, "for my own sake." God didn't do it for *your* sake, but for *His own* sake. "I will not remember your sins," He promised. If *God* doesn't remember them, why should you? You shouldn't!

When you were born again, you were redeemed from the penalty of sin. If you had to go on paying for your wrongdoing, you'd have to go to hell when you died, because that's part of the penalty too. However, thank God, we are redeemed not only from the *power* of sin, but also from the *penalty* of sin. Jesus took our place. He suffered the penalty of sin.

Confession: *When I repented, my heavenly Father blotted out my transgressions. He does not remember my sins. Therefore, I won't remember them either. And I won't remind Him of them.*

New Creation Facts

Be ye not unequally yoked together with unbelievers: for what fellowship hath righteousness with unrighteousness? and what communion hath light with darkness? And what concord hath Christ with Belial? or what part hath he that believeth with an infidel? And what agreement hath the temple of God with idols? . . .

— 2 CORINTHIANS 6:14-16

In order to have strong faith, you must see yourself as God sees you — and you must say about yourself what God says about you.

In the Scripture quoted above, believers are called *believers,* and unbelievers are called *unbelievers.* So you can call yourself a believer.

Believers are called *righteousness,* and unbelievers are called *unrighteousness.* Have you ever called yourself *righteousness?* That's what the Bible calls you, so you are.

Believers are called *light,* and unbelievers are called *darkness.*

"And what concord hath Christ with Belial?" Here the Church is identified with Christ. Christ is the Head, and we are the Body. Your head doesn't go by one name and your body by another, does it? The Church is identified with Christ — we are the Body of Christ. Think about it. Let it soak in. What a basis for faith!

Confession: *Because I am in Christ — I am a believer. I am righteousness. I am light. I am one who believes. I am the temple of God.*

19

God, Our Righteousness

Even the righteousness of God which is by faith of Jesus Christ unto all and upon all them that believe....
— ROMANS 3:22

To be a complete overcomer — to walk in the highest kind of faith — you must know the reality of your own righteousness in Christ.

Read Romans 3:21-26. Mark these Scriptures in your Bible. Think on them — feed on them — until they become a part of your inner-consciousness.

If your Bible is a *King James Version,* keep in mind that the same Greek word which is translated in verse 26 as "just" (and other forms thereof) can also be translated as "righteous." So you may substitute the word "righteous" for "just." Many translations read this way.

For example, *Young's Literal Translation of the Bible* translates Romans 3:26 this way: "for the shewing forth of His [God's] righteousness in the present time, for His being righteous, and declaring him righteous who is of the faith of Jesus."

What do these Scriptures tell us? That God Himself is righteous. And that God has declared us to be righteous because we have believed in Jesus.

Confession: *God the Father declared Himself righteous through Jesus Christ. And God the Father — my very own Father — declares me righteous, for I believe in Jesus. Therefore I am righteous. I am a recipient of the righteousness of God.*

Right Standing

For if by one man's offence death reigned by one; much more they which receive abundance of grace and of the gift of righteousness shall reign in life by one, Jesus Christ.
— ROMANS 5:17

For with the heart man believeth unto righteousness....
— ROMANS 10:10

Most people think righteousness is a state of spiritual development which you grow into by right living. The Bible teaches right living — but right living itself will never make you righteous. (If it would, you wouldn't need Jesus.)

Righteousness means rightness, or right standing, with God.

Righteousness is a gift. A gift is something you receive now — whole and complete. A fruit, on the other hand, is a state of spiritual development — something which grows and develops. Thank God, *we can grow spiritually — but we cannot grow in righteousness.* In fact, you won't be any more righteous when you get to heaven than you are right now.

How did you get to be righteous? You were born that way! Righteousness comes through the New Birth. With your heart you believed unto righteousness. When you were born again, you received the life and nature of God the Father (John 5:24,26; 2 Peter 1:4). God's nature makes you righteous!

Confession: *I have righteousness. It was given to me. I believed unto righteousness, and I received it at my New Birth. I have right standing with God. I am righteous.*

The Righteousness of God

For he hath made him to be sin for us, who knew no sin;
that we might be made the righteousness of God in him.

— 2 CORINTHIANS 5:21

"*For he hath made him to be sin for us, who knew no sin ....*"

I've tested people by reading this portion of Scripture and then I've asked them, "How many of you believe that's true?" They all lifted their hands.

Then I would read the last part of the same verse, "*... that we might be made the righteousness of God in him.*"

And then I would say to them, "Therefore, we — you and I — are the righteousness of God in Christ. How many of you believe that's true?"

Most of the time I couldn't get half the crowd to lift their hands on the last part. And yet, if the first part of that verse is true, then the last must be true too!

God made a provision for us that belongs to us. We need to realize that it is ours!

Confession: *Jesus became sin for me that I might become the righteousness of God in Him. I am the righteousness of God in Christ. God provided righteousness for me. Righteousness is mine. I have it now! I am righteous now.*

Reigning in Righteousness

For if, because of one man's trespass (lapse, offense) death reigned through that one, much more surely will those who receive [God's] overflowing grace (unmerited favor) and the free gift of righteousness (putting them into right standing with Himself) reign as kings in life through the One, Jesus Christ, the Messiah, the Anointed One.

— ROMANS 5:17 Amplified

One of our greatest problems is relegating everything to the future. Think about the songs we sing: "When we all get to heaven . . ." Thank God we are going to get there, but we don't have to wait until we get there to enjoy God's blessings. We can have them *now!*

Yes, we will reign with Christ *then*. But we don't have to wait until then! When does our text say we will reign as kings? Now! In life! In *this* life! How? By Jesus Christ!

Paul used this illustration of reigning as kings because in the day in which he lived, they had kings. Each king reigned over his own particular domain. His word was the final authority. What he said went! He ruled. He reigned.

The Word says that we reign in life by Christ Jesus Why? Because we have been made the righteousness of God in Christ.

Confession: *Because I have received the free gift of righteousness, which puts me into right standing with God, I reign in life through the One, Jesus Christ. I reign as a righteous king in my domain. What I say goes!*

Effectual Prayer

The effectual fervent prayer of a righteous man availeth much.
                                                    — JAMES 5:16

Jesus who is righteous became your Righteousness (1 Cor. 1:30). Your standing with God is secure. Therefore, you can stand in the presence of God as though you had never done wrong! As though you had never sinned! Without a sense of condemnation, and without a spiritual inferiority complex! No wonder Hebrews 4:16 says, *"Let us therefore come BOLDLY unto the throne of grace, that we may obtain mercy, and find grace to help in time of need."*

When you know these powerful spiritual truths, you won't have to run around to get somebody else to do your praying for you. You'll know that God the Father will hear you as quickly as He hears any other believer. Why? Because you have just as good a standing with God as any other Christian has. God doesn't love one member of His Body more than another.

People sometimes think, *If I could just get So-and-so to pray, his prayer would work. He's a real man of God.* No, that Christian may have learned how to take advantage of what belongs to him a little better than you have, but he's not any more righteous than you are. And God won't hear him pray any quicker than He will hear you pray.

Confession: *I am the righteousness of God in Christ. Because I am righteous, God hears me when I pray. And my prayers avail much.*

Provision

If we confess our sins, he is faithful and just to forgive us our sins, and to cleanse us from all unrighteousness.

— 1 JOHN 1:9

Someone asked me once, "I can see from the Scriptures that we've received remission from our past sins; that we've received the gift of righteousness; and that we've been made righteous new creatures. But what about those sins I've committed since I've become a Christian?"

Thank God for His provision — First John 1:9! This verse isn't for sinners — it's for Christians! First John is written to Christians (1 John 2:1,2).

When a man sins, he is under condemnation. He loses his sense of righteousness. But when he confesses to the Lord, "I have sinned; I have failed You. Forgive me, Lord, in Jesus' Name," the Lord does two things:

1. He forgives him
2. He cleanses him

What does God cleanse him from? All unrighteousness!

Unrighteousness is simply the word righteousness with the prefix "un" attached to it. When we are cleansed from *un*righteousness, or *non*righteousness, then we are righteous again! Praise the Lord!

Confession: *Thank You, Father, for your provision of First John 1:9. Thank You for your faithfulness in forgiving and cleansing me from all unrighteousness, that I may continually have right standing in your sight.*

Receiving the Holy Spirit

And they were all filled with the Holy Ghost....
— ACTS 2:4

... they sent unto them Peter and John: Who, when they were come down, prayed for them, that they might receive the Holy Ghost. — ACTS 8:14,15

... Have ye received the Holy Ghost since ye believed? — ACTS 19:2

In New Testament times, it was the exception for believers not to have received the indwelling of the Holy Spirit with the supernatural sign and initial evidence of speaking in tongues. The Epistles were written to believers who knew Jesus as Savior and who had been filled with the Holy Spirit.

Thank God, the Holy Spirit is in us too. But too often people who have been born again and then filled with the Spirit just think of themselves as having received a blessing or some kind of experience — and they miss entirely what the Word of God teaches! *A Divine Personality actually comes to live in us! God Himself in the Person of the Holy Spirit indwells us!*

Confession: *God Himself in the Person of the Holy Spirit indwells me. The Creator dwells in me. God lives in me.*

God-Inside

Do you not discern and understand that you [the whole
church at Corinth] are God's temple (His sanctuary), and
that God's Spirit has His permanent dwelling in you — to
be at home in you [collectively as a church and also
individually]?   — 1 CORINTHIANS 3:16 *Amplified*

God Himself, after He makes us new creatures,
actually makes our bodies His home. No longer
does He dwell in an earth-made Holy of Holies.
God says, *"What? know ye not that your body is*
the temple of the Holy Ghost which is in you . . . ?"
(1 Cor. 6:19).

We need to become mindful that we are the
temple of the Holy Spirit — we have God inside us!

Chiseled on the front of a beautiful church in
Texas is an Old Testament Scripture declaring
that this building is the temple of God. I get
provoked every time I drive by. Why? Because
these people have a lie right on the front of their
church building!

To say that a church building is the house of
God because He dwells there, is incorrect. God
doesn't dwell in a church building. If we mean that
a church building is the house of God because it
has been dedicated to God, that *is* correct. But we
must be careful not to confuse spiritual things
with natural things. Therefore, we must be careful
to state spiritual things as they really are.

Your *body* is the house or temple of God — not
the building where you worship. Remembering this
fact will help you in your obedience and in your
faith.

Confession: *My body is the temple of God. God has His*
permanent dwelling in me. God is at home in me.

The Greater One Within

Ye are of God, little children, and have overcome them:
because greater is he that is in you, than he that is in the
world. — 1 JOHN 4:4

It should be common practice for you to say in every crisis of life: *"I am a victor. I am more than a conqueror. The Creator dwells in me. The Greater One lives in me. He can put me over. The Greater One will make me a success. I can't fail!"*

That's not bragging on you; it's bragging on the Greater One who is in you. And it will put Him to work for you!

If you're a born-again, Spirit-filled believer, you have in you, ready for your use, everything you will ever need to put you over. The divine potential of all the power that there is, indwells you!

If you will believe the Bible and begin to confess what it says, the Greater One will rise up in you and give illumination to your mind, direction to your spirit, health to your body, and help in every aspect of life.

Confession: *Greater is He who is in me than he that is in the world. The Greater One is greater than the devil, greater than disease, greater than poverty, greater than death, greater than all the power of the enemy. And He lives in me! The Greater One can make me a success. I cannot fail!*

Ability

. . . for ye are the temple of the living God; as God hath said, I will dwell in them, and walk in them; and I will be their God, and they shall be my people.

— 2 CORINTHIANS 6:16

Few Christians seem to be conscious of the fact that God lives in them. They couldn't be and still talk the way they do.

What do I mean? When a need arises in their life, some Christians are quick to say, "No, I can't do that." Why? Because they're trusting in themselves, or the flesh, to put them over. They know they don't have the ability in themselves to do it.

But if we are conscious that God is in us, then we know He has the ability to do *anything*. So we can stop saying, "I can't," and we can begin saying with confidence, "I *can* — because I'm trusting God! I *can* — because God is in me! I *can* — because greater is He that is in me than he that is in the world!"

No matter what you face — and you may be facing seemingly impossible obstacles in your life — you can say, "God will put me over! He'll make me a success! The Greater One indwells me!"

That's scriptural believing. That's faith talking. And it will put the Greater One to work for you!

Confession: *The Spirit of God indwells me. I trust the Indwelling One. He has the ability. I can do all things — because the Spirit of God is in me. I can — because He has all ability.*

Helper

And I will ask the Father, and He will give you another Comforter (Counselor, Helper, Intercessor, Advocate, Strengthener and Standby) that He may remain with you forever. — JOHN 14:16 *Amplified*

It is sad to realize that some Christians ignore the Holy Spirit who is dwelling within them. I believe they mistakenly think He will come in, take control of their lives, and make them do whatever needs to be done automatically with no effort on their part — but He won't. Demons do that. They are the ones that make people do things which the people don't want to do. Demons drive, force, and control people.

The Holy Spirit, on the other hand, is a Gentleman. He will never force you to do anything against your will. In the Scriptures we see that the Holy Spirit leads, guides, prompts, and urges. He may give you a gentle "push," but He will never *force* you to act.

Some complain, "Why doesn't God do this or that?" The Holy Spirit won't do anything until you put Him to work for you! He is sent to be your Helper. He is not sent to do the job for you, but to *help you* do it.

When you know the Holy Spirit is in you, then you can act on God's Word intelligently, and the Holy Spirit will work through you. Begin to talk in line with today's confession, and you will find that He who indwells you will become more real to you.

Confession: *The Greater One is in me. I'm depending on Him. He will live big in me. He will help me. The Greater One will put me over. He will make me a success!*

The Same Spirit

But if the Spirit of him that raised up Jesus from the dead dwell in you, he that raised up Christ from the dead shall also quicken your mortal bodies by his Spirit that dwelleth in you.
— ROMANS 8:11

The term "mortal bodies" in this text does not refer to our resurrected bodies in the *future;* it refers to our mortal bodies *now!* (Mortal means death doomed.) Our bodies will not be mortal in the grave. They are mortal *now.* The Spirit will not dwell in them then. The Spirit of God dwells in them *now.* Now is when we need our mortal bodies quickened by God's Spirit which dwells in us.

One of the reasons for the Holy Spirit's indwelling our mortal bodies is to heal us of the diseases which are continually trying to attach themselves to us.

Healing is part of God's plan or covenant for us today. Healing is part of His provision for His children — His Body — upon the earth.

If we could understand God's plan of healing as we ought to understand it, the sick would simply be healed the moment sickness tried to touch them!

Confession: *The same Spirit that raised Christ from the dead dwells in me. He lives in me. He quickens my mortal body. He heals my mortal body.*

His Permanent Home

May He grant you out of the rich treasury of His glory to be strengthened and reinforced with mighty power in the inner man by the (Holy) Spirit [Himself] — indwelling your innermost being and personality. May Christ through your faith [actually] dwell — settle down, abide, make His permanent home — in your hearts! ...

— EPHESIANS 3:16,17 *Amplified*

How does Christ actually dwell, settle down, and make His permanent home in your heart? *Through your faith.*

That's what God wants to do: Make His permanent home in your heart! But that's what Christians haven't allowed Him to do! (Remember: This Scripture was written to born-again, Spirit-filled Christians.)

Christians sing, "Come by here, Lord, come by here," implying that the Lord's not here — but *if* we could just get Him to come by, He might do something for us. And we sing, "Reach out and touch the Lord as He passes by." All of these sentiments are based on physical sense knowledge. I don't have to reach out and touch the Lord, because He lives in me! And we sing, "Just to have a touch, O Lord, from You." What do I want with *touches* when I've got the Holy Spirit living inside me?

Trust God who already dwells within you! Learn to become "God-inside-minded"!

Confession: *I am strengthened and reinforced with mighty power in my inner man by the Holy Spirit indwelling my innermost being. Christ actually dwells, settles down, abides, and makes His permanent home in my heart!*

Fellowship

God is faithful, by whom ye were called unto the fellowship of his Son Jesus Christ our Lord.

— 1 CORINTHIANS 1:9

The highest honor God has conferred upon you is to be a joint-fellowshipper with God the Father, His Son, and the Holy Spirit in carrying out God's plan for the redemption of the human race.

By virtue of the New Birth, you became related to the Creator of the universe! You became God's child. You have a relationship with Him. But relationship without fellowship is a lifeless thing. It's like marriage without love or fellowship.

Fellowship with God is the mother of faith. And God has called you individually into fellowship with His Son.

Confession: *God has called me into fellowship with His Son, Jesus Christ. I will walk in fellowship and communion with Jesus. I will talk with Jesus. I will work with Jesus. I am a joint-fellowshipper with God the Father, with Jesus Christ, and with the Holy Spirit in carrying out God's great plan of redemption for the human race.*

Fellowship in Prayer

That which we have seen and heard declare we unto you, that ye also may have fellowship with us: and truly our fellowship is with the Father, and with his Son Jesus Christ. And these things write we unto you, that your joy may be full. . . . But if we walk in the light, as he is in the light, we have fellowship one with another, and the blood of Jesus Christ his Son cleanseth us from all sin.

— 1 JOHN 1:3,4,7

If you have fellowship with God, and you're walking in the light as He is in the light, then prayer becomes one of the greatest assets you have inherited in Christ.

Prayer is joining forces with God the Father. It is fellowshipping with Him. It is carrying out His will upon the earth.

Prayer should never be a problem or a burden to you. It should be a joy! Prayer — real prayer — won't take anything *out* of you; it will always put something *into* you! Because you are fellowshipping with God when you pray.

Confession: *I have fellowship with my Father in prayer. And my joy is full! I fellowship with God. I commune with God — I talk with Him, and I listen to Him — that I may carry out His will upon the earth.*

Joining Forces

What shall we then say to these things? If God be for us, who can be against us? He that spared not his own Son, but delivered him up for us all, how shall he not with him also freely give us all things? — ROMANS 8:31,32

God and you are working together in carrying out His plan for the redemption of the world. God can't get along without you anymore than you can get along without Him. That's one reason why Jesus gave us the illustration of the vine and the branches. The vine can't bear fruit without the branches, and the branches can't live without the vine.

Our text today is a part of the conclusion of the first eight chapters of Romans. And this passage shows us the absolute oneness of the Father God with His children. It shows us the perfect fellowship and cooperation God's children enjoy with their heavenly Father. It shows the mastery God's children have over the forces of darkness and circumstances. And God climaxes this passage with verse 37: *"Nay, in all these things we are more than conquerors through him that loved us."*

God is working actively on your behalf. He is standing up for you. He is fighting for you. He is supplying all your needs. Out of the treasury of His abundant grace, He is giving you His wisdom and His ability!

Confession: *God is for me! Who can be against me? I am one with my Father! He is active on my behalf. He supplies my needs. I fellowship and cooperate with Him!*

Sufficiency

And such trust have we through Christ to God-ward: Not that we are sufficient of ourselves to think any thing as of ourselves; but our sufficiency is of God; Who also hath made us able ministers of the new testament [New Covenant]. . . .   — 2 CORINTHIANS 3:4-6

We aren't ordinary people.
We're tied up with Omnipotence.
We're united with God Himself.
We're carrying out God's will here on the earth.
We're the channels through whom God is pouring Himself out upon the world.

It is perfectly normal, then, that God should become our sufficiency — that His ability should become our ability.

Now we can better understand First Corinthians 3:9, *"For we are labourers together with God. . . ."* That's fellowship with the Father! He supplies strength, wisdom, grace, and ability — the supernatural tools with which we work as able ministers of the New Covenant.

Confession: *My sufficiency is of God, who makes me an able minister of the New Covenant. God is my sufficiency. He is my ability. I am a laborer together with God in carrying out His will upon the earth.*

The Name

And Jesus came and spake unto them, saying, ALL POWER
[authority] *IS GIVEN UNTO ME in heaven and in earth.*
GO YE THEREFORE....

— MATTHEW 28:18,19

And these signs shall follow them that believe; IN MY
NAME.... — MARK 16:17

What effect would it have on your life if a
wealthy man were to give you a legal document,
telling you to use it to supply every one of your
needs?

Yet we have been given something even greater
than that! God has given us the power of attorney
to use the Name of Jesus! And that Name has
authority in this earth. The use of that Name is
not a matter of faith, actually, but rather it is a
matter of assuming your legal rights in Christ,
taking your place as a son of God, and using what
belongs to you. His Name belongs to you!

We have a right to use that Name against our
enemies. We have a right to use that Name in our
praise and worship. We have a right to use that
Name in our petitions. Praise God, that Name
belongs to us!

That Name has been given to us that we might
carry out the will of God the Father in this dispen-
sation in which we live. The Early Church used this
authority. They acted for Jesus in His stead. And
we are to use His Name and act in His stead today!

Confession: *All authority in heaven and earth resides in*
the Name of Jesus. The use of that Name and its authority
have been given to me. I have a right to use the Name of
Jesus!

The Father Glorified

And whatsoever ye shall ask IN MY NAME, that will I do,
that the Father may be glorified in the Son.

— JOHN 14:13

What a striking promise!

When we are born into the family of God, the right and privilege to use the Name of Jesus is given to us by the New Birth. All authority vested in that Name is given to us so that the Father may be glorified in the Son.

The Son was an outcast on the earth. He hung naked before the world and was crucified. But wherever the shame of the crucifixion has been preached, the might, power, and honor of His Name also has gone — shedding blessings upon the human race and bringing glory to God the Father.

Jesus' Name is to take Jesus' place upon the earth. All Jesus could do during His earth walk can now be done by every believer. Jesus is in that Name. Jesus *is* that Name. All Jesus was — all He did — all He is — all He will ever be — is in that Name now!

When we use Jesus' Name, we bring onto the scene the fullness of His finished work at Calvary. By our use of that Name, the living, healing Christ is present — to the glory of God the Father!

Confession: *I will use the Name of Jesus, as directed by His Word, to bring glory to God the Father.*

Faith Demonstrated

And Jesus answering saith unto them, Have faith in God.
— MARK 11:22

The margin of a good *King James* reference Bible renders today's text as, "Have the faith of God." Greek scholars tell us the literal translation of what Jesus said here is, "Have the God-kind of faith." Some modern translations also show the verse this way.

Even if you don't know anything about Greek, you can readily see that this would be a correct translation of this verse, because Jesus had just demonstrated to the disciples that He had that kind of faith: the God-kind of faith, the kind of faith that God used to create the world in the beginning.

Earlier in this chapter, Jesus had spoken to the barren fig tree. He hadn't prayed. He had simply said to that tree, "*. . . No man eat fruit of thee hereafter for ever*" (v. 14).

The next morning, as Jesus and the disciples passed by the same place, they saw that the fig tree had dried up from its roots. Peter, remembering, said, "*. . . Master, behold, the fig tree which thou cursedst is withered away*" (v. 21).

Jesus answered him, "Have the God-kind of faith."

Jesus demonstrated the God-kind of faith for us. Then He told us to have it.

Confession: *I see the demonstration of the God-kind of faith by my Lord Jesus Christ. Jesus expects me to know about and to have the God-kind of faith! And I do have it!*

Faith Defined

For verily I say unto you, That whosoever shall say unto this mountain, Be thou removed, and be thou cast into the sea; and shall not doubt in his heart, but shall believe that those things which he saith shall come to pass; he shall have whatsoever he saith.
— MARK 11:23

Just after Jesus had demonstrated the God-kind of faith, He defined it. Mark 11:23 is Jesus' definition of the God-kind of faith. He described it as the kind of faith in which (1) A person believes in his heart, (2) Then, a person says with his mouth what he believes in his heart, (3) And, it comes to pass.

God used that kind of faith to create the world in the beginning. God believed that what He said would come to pass! So He said, "Let there be an earth." And there was an earth. In fact, He created everything — the sun, the moon, the stars, the plants and animals — everything except man — by believing what He said would come to pass. Then God said it. And it came to pass. That is the God-kind of faith!

Confession: *"Whosoever shall say...." includes me. What I believe in my heart, and say with my mouth, shall come to pass. I live and operate in the God-kind of faith.*

Faith Dealt

For I say, through the grace given unto me, to every man that is among you, not to think of himself more highly than he ought to think; but to think soberly, according as God hath dealt to every man the measure of faith.

— ROMANS 12:3

"Faith — that's what I want!" many people say to me. "And I'm praying that God will give it to me."

If that's what you're doing, you're wasting your time. It would do no more good to pray that God will give you faith than it would to twiddle your thumbs and recite "Twinkle, Twinkle, Little Star." Praying for faith is lost motion and wasted time, because every believer already has a measure of the God-kind of faith. You don't have to get it. You don't have to pray for it. You don't have to fast for it. You don't have to promise to do better and be good to get it. You already have it!

Paul wasn't writing to sinners, but to believers, in this verse in Romans. He said, *"I say . . . to every man that is among you* [not to every man in the world], *. . . God hath dealt to every man the measure of faith."*

All believers have faith! God gave it to them!

Confession: *God dealt to me the measure of faith. I have a measure of the God-kind of faith! God already gave it to me! I have it now!*

Saved Through Faith!

For by grace are ye saved through faith; and that not of yourselves: it is the gift of God. — EPHESIANS 2:8

Notice that the faith you are saved by is "not of yourselves." In other words, it's not a natural, human faith. It's the gift of God! That agrees with Romans 12:3, which states that "*. . . God hath dealt to every man the measure of faith.*"

Yet Christians will say, "I just don't have any faith."

I always answer by saying, "Then why don't you get saved? Saved people have faith! You can't be saved without faith."

All believers have faith. The Bible says they do! But many Christians don't realize they do — and they're not using the faith they have. They "take sides" against God, against the Bible, and against themselves, without recognizing what they are doing, by continually talking about how they don't have faith.

God's Word is God speaking. God and His Word are one: If God's Word says something, that is God saying it. And God's Word says that God has dealt to you the measure of faith. It has to be the God-kind of faith — because that's the only kind of faith God has!

Confession: *I am saved! And I was saved by grace through faith — the gift of God! I have a measure of the God-kind of faith! I have a measure of the kind of faith which created the world in the beginning! I have a measure of mountain-moving faith!*

How Faith Comes

So then faith cometh by hearing, and hearing by the word of God.

— ROMANS 10:17

How does God give the sinner faith to be saved?

Let me read along with you from the tenth chapter of Romans, which talks about salvation and about getting faith to be saved. (My comments are in brackets.)

"But what saith it? The word is nigh thee, even in thy mouth, and in thy heart: that is, the word of faith, which we preach [Notice that God's Word is called 'the word of faith.' That's because it builds faith. It causes faith to come into the hearts of those who are open to it.]; *That if thou shalt confess with thy mouth the Lord Jesus, and shalt believe in thine heart that God hath raised him from the dead, thou shalt be saved. For with the heart man believeth unto righteousness; and with the mouth confession is made unto salvation. . . . For whosoever shall call upon the name of the Lord shall be saved. How then shall they call on him in whom they have not believed?* [Now get this.] *and how shall they believe in him of whom they have not heard? . . . So then faith cometh by hearing, and hearing by the word of God"* (Rom. 10:8-10,13,14,17).

You cannot believe without hearing. Faith comes by hearing. Hearing what? The Word of God!

Confession: *I listen to the Word of God. And faith comes to me.*

The Word of Faith

But what saith it? The word is nigh thee, even in thy mouth, and in thy heart: that is, the word of faith, which we preach.
— ROMANS 10:8

God's Word is called *"the word of faith."*

Faith is based on facts — the facts of God's Word.

Unbelief is founded on theories. This is my definition of a theory: "A theory is a supposition established upon ignorance of the subject under discussion." The reason why many churches are full of unbelief is because they've heard too much theory. The ministry has thrived on a psychology of unbelief, and the poor, dear church members are simply a product of what they have heard their ministers preach.

The best way to really help people is to tell them what the Bible says — to give them what God's Word says — not what some man says. Man can be wrong, but God can never be wrong.

No matter what the circumstances — no matter what has happened in your life — God's Word has something to say on the subject. Find out what God's Word says. Faith will come — and it will change things for you.

Confession: *The Word . . . God's Word . . . the word of faith . . . is near me. I hide it in my heart. I speak it with my mouth. It produces faith. And faith changes things.*

The Same Faith

We having the same spirit of faith, according as it is written, I believed, and therefore have I spoken: we also believe, and therefore speak.

— 2 CORINTHIANS 4:13

Paul wrote, *"We HAVING the same spirit of faith...."*

He didn't say, "trying to have," or "praying for," or "hoping for"; he said, "having"! Having what? The same spirit of faith. And what kind of faith is that? The kind that (1) believes, and (2) therefore speaks.

Isn't that the same kind of faith Jesus is talking about in Mark 11:23? The kind that (1) believes in the heart, (2) says with the mouth, and (3) then it comes to pass?

Yes! That's the same spirit of faith! And Second Corinthians 4:13 says that we have it!

Confession: *I have the same spirit of faith. I believe and therefore I speak. I have a measure of the God-kind of faith. I have a measure of the kind of faith that created the worlds in the beginning. I have a measure of mountain-moving faith.*

Growing Faith

We are bound to thank God always for you, brethren, as it is meet, because that your faith groweth exceedingly....
— 2 THESSALONIANS 1:3

God gets all believers started off equally with *the measure* of faith after they are born again. He doesn't give one baby Christian more faith than He gives another. After we are born again, however, it is up to each of us to develop the measure of faith that has been given to us.

Too many have done with their faith what the fellow did with his one talent: He wrapped it in a napkin, hid it, and didn't use it.

Your measure of faith can be increased — it can grow. But *you* are the one who increases it — not God!

Your measure of faith can be increased by doing these two things: (1) Feeding it on the Word of God, and (2) Exercising it by putting it into practice.

Confession: *God has given me the measure of faith. I will see to it that my faith grows exceedingly. I will feed my faith on the Word of God. I will exercise my faith — I will put it into practice. My faith is growing.*

Faith Is Measurable

When Jesus heard it, he marvelled, and said to them that followed, Verily I say unto you, I have not found so great faith, no, not in Israel. — MATTHEW 8:10

A centurion came to Jesus on behalf of his sick servant. When Jesus said, *"I will come and heal him"* (Matt. 8:7), the centurion answered, *". . . speak the word only, and my servant shall be healed"* (v. 8).

Jesus said to him, *". . . Go thy way; and as thou hast believed, so be it done unto thee"* (v. 13).

Turning to His disciples, Jesus said, *". . . I have not found so GREAT faith, no, not in Israel"* (v. 10). Therefore, it is possible for a person to develop great faith.

On the other hand, an example of little faith is seen when Peter began to sink after having walked on the water. Jesus chided Peter, saying, *". . . O thou of LITTLE faith, wherefore didst thou doubt?"* (Matt. 14:31).

If faith can be *great,* and faith can be *little,* then faith is *measurable!*

Here are some Scriptures that prove faith is measurable: Growing faith (2 Thess. 1:3) . . . weak faith (Rom. 4:19) . . . strong faith (Rom. 4:20) . . . rich faith (James 2:5) . . . full of faith (Acts 6:5) . . . perfect faith (James 2:22) . . . unfeigned faith (1 Tim. 1:5) . . . shipwrecked faith (1 Tim. 1:19) . . . overcoming faith (1 John 5:4).

Confession: *My faith is growing. My faith is measuring up to great faith, strong faith, rich faith, perfect faith, unfeigned faith, overcoming faith. I am full of faith!*

Faith Food

But he answered and said, It is written, Man shall not live by bread alone, but by every word that proceedeth out of the mouth of God.

— MATTHEW 4:4

Here, Jesus is using a natural human term to convey a spiritual thought. He is saying that what bread, or food, is to the body, the Word of God is to the spirit, or heart, of man.

You can feed your spirit. You can feed your faith. God's Word is *faith food.*

Smith Wigglesworth, the great English preacher under whose ministry fourteen people were reportedly raised from the dead, is called an apostle of faith. He said, "I never consider myself thoroughly dressed unless I have my Testament in my pocket. I would as soon go out without my shoes as without my Bible!"

In Wigglesworth's travels over the world, he stayed in many homes. People have reported that after every meal, even in restaurants, he would always push back from the table, get out his Testament, and say, "We have fed the body; now let's feed the inward man." Then Wigglesworth would read something about faith, usually winding up giving a little faith message.

Confession: *I live by every Word of God. I feed my faith. I feed my inward man. I feed on faith food — God's Word!*

A Demand

But without faith it is impossible to please him: for he that cometh to God must believe that he is, and that he is a rewarder of them that diligently seek him.

— HEBREWS 11:6

God demands faith of us.

Now, if God demands that we have faith when it is impossible for us to have faith, then we have a right to challenge His justice. But if God places in our hands the means whereby faith can be produced, then the responsibility is up to us as to whether we have faith or not.

God has given us His Word, and He has told us that "*. . . faith cometh by hearing, and hearing by the word of God*" (Rom. 10:17).

F. F. Bosworth, an authority on healing and the author of the classic book *Christ the Healer,* said, "Most Christians feed their bodies three hot meals a day, their spirits one cold snack a week, and then wonder why they are so weak in faith."

Confession: *I will please my heavenly Father. I will walk in faith. I will feed my faith regularly on the faith food God has put into my hands.*

Exercise

. . . According to your faith be it unto you.
— MATTHEW 9:29

If you eat natural food regularly and get no exercise, you'll grow fat and flabby. Likewise, if you don't exercise your faith, your "faith muscles" will be flabby.

Exercise your faith on the level where you are. Some Christians are beyond others in the development of their faith. As you feed and exercise your faith, it will grow. Remember, nobody climbs a ladder by starting on the top rung!

Some people have become defeated because they tried to believe *beyond* their level of faith. They heard faith taught, and they tried to start at the top of the ladder. Because their faith wasn't at that level, faith didn't work for them, and they said, "That faith message doesn't work. I tried it, but it doesn't work."

Faith will work for you as you exercise it. After a while you'll be able to believe God for things you never dreamed you could. According to your faith be it unto you. If your request is based on God's Word, and you believe God to do it, God will do it.

Wherever you are in faith, keep your attitude right. Keep a positive attitude — and keep the switch of faith turned on. Keep believing God and using your faith.

Confession: *According to my faith be it unto me. I am using my faith today. I am exercising my faith. I am putting my faith into practice. I see to it that my faith is always at work!*

Faith's Location

For with the heart man believeth. . . .

— ROMANS 10:10

. . . and shall not doubt in his heart, but shall believe. . . .

— MARK 11:23

Faith — real faith, Bible faith, scriptural faith — is of the heart, not the head.

What does it mean to believe with the heart? What is the heart of man?

Well, it's not the physical organ that pumps blood through your body and keeps you alive. You couldn't believe with your physical heart any more than you could believe with your physical hand, eye, ear, nose, or foot!

Consider how we use the term "heart" today. When we talk about the "heart" of a tree, we mean the center, the very core, of the tree. When we talk about the "heart" of a subject, we mean the most important part of that subject; the very center of it; the main part around which the rest revolves.

Likewise, when God speaks of man's "heart," He is speaking about the main part of the man — the very center of man's being — his spirit!

Confession: *With my heart I believe God. I do not doubt in my heart. I believe in my heart.*

The Hidden Man

*But let it be the hidden man of the heart, in that which
is not corruptible, even the ornament of a meek and quiet
spirit, which is in the sight of God of great price.*

— 1 PETER 3:4

*For which cause we faint not; but though our outward man
perish, yet the inward man is renewed day by day.*

— 2 CORINTHIANS 4:16

Let's allow God to tell us what the heart is. In
First Peter 3:4, God says that the heart is a man
— a *hidden* man.

That is, this hidden man is hidden to the
physical senses. You can't see him with your
physical eye, nor feel him with your physical hand.
That's because he is not a physical being; he is the
"inward man" spoken of in Second Corinthians
4:16.

These two expressions found in Scripture give
us God's definition of the human spirit: "The
inward man" and "the hidden man of the heart."

Confession: *I believe God from the hidden man of my heart.
I believe God from my inward man. I believe God from my
spirit.*

Spirit Being

And the very God of peace sanctify you wholly; and I pray God your whole spirit and soul and body be preserved blameless unto the coming of our Lord Jesus Christ.

— 1 THESSALONIANS 5:23

You *are* a spirit.
You *have* a soul,
And you *live* in a body.

With your *spirit* you contact the spiritual world.

With your *body* you contact the physical world.

And with your *soul* you contact the intellectual world.

These are the only three realms you contact. There are no more.

Man is a spirit being who was created in the image of God, who is a Spirit. (*See* Genesis 1:26; John 4:24.)

You, too, are a spirit being. And it will help your faith to think like that, because faith is of the heart, or the spirit, or the inward man. (The terms "spirit" of man and "heart" of man are used interchangeably throughout the Bible.) Faith is not of the head. Faith is not of the body. *Faith is of the heart!*

Confession: *I am a spirit. I have a soul. And I live in a body. I am a spirit being created in the image of God. With my spirit I contact God. With my spirit I believe God!*

Heart vs. Head

Trust in the Lord with all thine heart; and lean not unto thine own understanding. — PROVERBS 3:5

Your own understanding is simply your own mental processes — your own human thinking. In other words, we could read this verse, "Trust in the Lord with all thine heart; and lean not unto thine own head."

Faith will work in your heart with doubt in your head! Many Christians are defeated because when a doubt enters their minds, they say, "I'm doubting." But Jesus didn't say, ". . . and shall not doubt in his *head.*" Jesus said, "*. . . and shall not doubt in his* heart, *but shall believe . . .*" (Mark 11:23). It's heart faith that gets the job done — not head faith.

Some of the greatest miracles that have ever happened in my life came when I began to make such faith statements as, "I believe from my heart that I receive my healing" — even though my *head* was saying, "It's not so. It's not so!" (And I was healed of two serious organic heart problems and an incurable blood disease in my almost totally paralyzed body.)

Do you ever have trouble with your head? Then just trust in the Lord with all your heart (not your head), and lean not unto your own understanding!

Confession: *I trust in the Lord with all my heart. I do not lean to my own understanding. I believe from my heart that what God's Word says is true.*

Head Faith

The other disciples therefore said unto him, We have seen the Lord. But he [Thomas] *said unto them, Except I shall see in his hands the print of the nails, and put my finger into the print of the nails, and thrust my hand into his side, I will not believe. And after eight days . . . came Jesus, the doors being shut, and stood in the midst, and said, Peace be unto you. Then saith he to Thomas, Reach hither thy finger, and behold my hands; and reach hither thy hand, and thrust it into my side: and BE NOT FAITHLESS, BUT BELIEVING. And Thomas answered and said unto him, My Lord and my God. Jesus saith unto him, Thomas, because thou hast seen me, thou hast believed: BLESSED ARE THEY THAT HAVE NOT SEEN, AND YET HAVE BELIEVED.* — JOHN 20:25-29

Thomas' faith was head faith. And Jesus did not commend Thomas for it. Jesus said, "You have believed because you have seen." Anyone can have that kind of faith, whether he be saint or sinner. That's head faith. Head faith is believing what your physical senses tell you.

Jesus commended heart faith. He said, *". . . blessed are they that have not seen, and yet have believed."* To believe with the heart means to believe apart from what your physical body or physical senses may indicate. The physical man believes what he sees with his physical eyes, hears with his physical ears, or feels with his physical senses. But the heart, on the other hand, believes in the Word of God regardless of what the physical senses say.

Confession: *I am not faithless; I am believing. I believe according to what God's Word says, regardless of what I see, hear, or feel.*

Heart Faith

Who against hope BELIEVED in hope, that he [Abraham]
*might become the father of many nations, ACCORDING
TO THAT WHICH WAS SPOKEN, So shall thy seed be.*
— ROMANS 4:18

Read Romans 4 for God's own account of
Abraham and his faith. Here, the eighteenth verse
says that Abraham believed. What did Abraham
believe? He believed "*. . . according to that which
was spoken. . . .*"

Abraham did not believe according to what he
could see. Abraham did not believe according to
what he could feel. Abraham did not believe
according to what his physical senses told him.
Abraham did not even believe according to what
his mind told him. Abraham believed according to
what was spoken by God!

Knowing this Scripture has brought me though
many hard places. When opposition and contra-
dicting circumstances have said, "No, you don't
have it," I've just stood my ground. When my feel-
ings have said, "No, you don't have it," I've just
stood my ground. When my sight said, "No, you
don't have it," I've just stood my ground. I've said
from my heart, "I believe according to that which
is spoken."

And "that which is spoken" is God's Word!

Confession: *I believe according to that which is spoken.
I believe according to that which is written. I am not moved
by what I see. I am not moved by what I feel. I am moved
only by what I believe!*

As Though They Were

(As it is written, I have made thee a father of many nations,)
before him whom he believed, even God, who quickeneth
the dead, and calleth those things which be not as though
they were.   — ROMANS 4:17

If Abraham believed according to what was
spoken, exactly what *was* spoken? What did
Abraham believe?

When Abram (as he was then called) was 99
years old, the Lord said to him, *"Neither shall thy
name any more be called Abram, but thy name
shall be Abraham; for a father of many nations
have I made thee"* (Gen. 17:5). Notice that God
did not say, "I'm *going to* do it"; He said, "I *have
made* thee."

When God made Abraham that promise,
Abraham was childless. But Abraham was told he
was not to believe he was "going to be" (future
tense) a father. (Those who are always "going to"
get something never get it. It is the same with the
ones who say, "I'm going to get saved sometime."
Or, "I'm going to get my healing sometime.")

No, faith is always present tense! Abraham had
to believe he "was made" the father of many
nations.

For, you see, faith calleth those things which
be not as though they were. That's what causes
them to come into being!

Confession: *Like my heavenly Father, I call those things*
which be not as though they were. And they come into
being! They're mine. I have them now!

Imitators of God

Therefore be imitators of God — copy Him and follow His example — as well-beloved children [imitate their father].
— **EPHESIANS 5:1** *Amplified*

"I'm not going to believe I've got something I don't see!" one preacher said to me.

"Do you believe you have any brains?" I replied.

"Certainly," he said.

"Have you ever seen them?"

Abraham believed something he couldn't see. Thomas refused to believe something he couldn't see. Thomas' name isn't listed in the gallery of heroes of faith in Hebrews 11. But Abraham's name is.

Another person once said to me, "Well, it would be all right for God to call those things which be not as though they were, because He's God. But it would be wrong for me to do that."

If it's wrong for *you* to do it, it's wrong for *God* to do it! Children of the devil act like the devil. Children of God are to act like God. God is a faith God. And we are faith children of a faith God. Because we are faith children of a faith God, we are to act in faith. And faith calls those things which be not as though they were!

Confession: *I am the faith child of a faith God. I imitate God, my Father. I follow His example as His well-beloved child. I act in faith. I call those things which be not as though they were. And they become.*

Strong Faith

He [Abraham] *staggered not at the promise of God through unbelief; but was strong in faith, giving glory to God; And being fully persuaded that, what he had promised, he was able also to perform.* — ROMANS 4:20,21

"I'm weak in faith," one woman said to me. "Will you pray that I'll grow stronger in faith?"

"No," I said. "I won't. To tell the truth, you are *strong* in faith! You just don't know it. May I ask you some questions?"

"Yes, of course," she said.

"Are you fully persuaded — fully persuaded — that what God has promised He is able to perform?"

"Certainly," she said. "I know God can do anything He said He would do. And I know He will do it."

"Can you say, 'Glory to God,' and praise God for His promises?"

"Certainly I can. I do that every day."

"Then you are strong in faith," I said, "according to Romans 4:20,21."

Abraham, too, was strong in faith. What is strong faith? Giving glory to God. And being fully persuaded that what God has promised He is able also to perform. If you can meet these two requirements, then you are strong in faith too.

Confession: *I am fully persuaded that what God has promised, He is able to perform. I can give glory to God. I am strong in faith. I have the Abraham-kind of faith. I have a measure of the God-kind of faith.*

Unforgiveness

And when ye stand praying, forgive, if ye have ought against any: that your Father also which is in heaven may forgive you your trespasses.

— MARK 11:25

Jesus had just made those marvelous, thrilling, amazing, astounding statements recorded in Mark 11:23 and 24. (And no one has ever yet plumbed the depths of those statements.)

But at the same time — at the same scene — and with the same breath — Jesus said, *"And when ye stand praying, forgive...."*

If there is an air of unforgiveness about you, your faith won't work! Your prayers won't work!

Unforgiveness is the only hindrance to faith that Jesus ever mentioned. Therefore, the subject of unforgiveness must be of primary importance. (If my prayers and my faith didn't work, the area of unforgiveness would be the first place I'd examine in my life.)

However, I never permit any unforgiveness about anyone to enter into my mind at all. I refuse to think about anything evil. I refuse to be resentful toward anyone. No matter what they have done to me — no matter what they have said about me — I will not permit it to affect me.

Confession: *My prayers work. My faith works. I do not permit unforgiveness into my being. I refuse to have ought against anyone.*

Forgiveness

But if ye do not forgive, neither will your Father which is in heaven forgive your trespasses.

— MARK 11:26

"Brother Hagin," a woman once said, "cast this old, unforgiving spirit out of me. I've got something against a woman here at church, and I can't forgive her. I don't seem to have the ability to forgive."

I replied, "Do you ever have to forgive your husband?"

"Oh, yes. I have to forgive him, and he has to forgive me."

"I thought you said you didn't have the ability to forgive."

She laughed and said, "I can forgive, can't I?"

"Certainly," I said. "If you can forgive one person, you can forgive another."

She understood and replied, "I can forgive. I do forgive. That's it!"

And it's just that simple. Don't complicate forgiveness. Jesus said, "When ye stand praying, forgive." That means we can forgive. Jesus didn't ask us to do something we can't do.

Confession: *I can forgive. I am quick to forgive. And my Father in heaven forgives me.*

Heart Love

. . . the love of God is shed abroad in our hearts by the Holy Ghost which is given unto us. — ROMANS 5:5

"I hate my mother-in-law!" a minister's wife once told me. "I don't even know if I'm saved or not, because the Bible says, *'Whosoever hateth his brother is a murderer: and ye know that no murderer hath eternal life abiding in him'* " (1 John 3:15).

I knew this woman was saved and filled with the Holy Spirit. But I also knew that she was letting the devil dominate her through her mind and her flesh.

So I said, "Look me in the eye and say out loud, 'I hate my mother-in-law.' As you're saying this, check up on the inside of you — because the love of God has been shed abroad in our *hearts,* not our *heads* — and tell me what is happening."

She did what I had asked and said, surprised, "Something is 'scratching' me down in my spirit!"

"Yes, something on the inside of you is trying to get your attention," I told her. "The love of God in your spirit wants to dominate you, but you are allowing your mind — where those thoughts have built up — to dominate you. In your heart, you actually love everyone."

"Yes, I do," she agreed. "What shall I do now?"

"Act in love. And let your heart dominate you — not your head."

Confession: *I let the love of God shed abroad in my heart by the Holy Spirit dominate me.*

Faith Released

For verily I say unto you, That whosoever shall SAY unto this mountain, Be thou removed, and be thou cast into the sea; and shall not doubt in his heart, but shall believe that those things which he SAITH shall come to pass; he shall have whatsoever he saith.

— MARK 11:23

Years ago, after spending an entire day in a church sanctuary praying, waiting on God, and reading and meditating on His Word, I lay down on the carpeting in front of the altar. I had come to the place where my mind was quiet. About that time, the Lord spoke to me in my spirit in as clear a voice as I'd ever heard.

He said, "Did you ever notice in the eleventh chapter of Mark, the twenty-third verse, that the word 'say' is included three times in some form, and the word 'believe' is used only once?"

I arose to a seated position and replied aloud, "No, I never noticed that!" (And there's no telling how many hundreds of times I had quoted that verse.)

Then the Lord said, "My people are not missing it primarily in their believing. They are missing it in their saying. They have been taught to believe, but *faith must be released in words through your mouth. You can have what you say.*" He added, "You will have to do three times as much teaching about the saying part as the believing part to get people to see this."

Confession: *I have what I say. I release my faith in words.*

What I Say

For verily I say unto you, That whosoever shall say unto this mountain, Be thou removed, and be thou cast into the sea; and shall not doubt in his heart, but shall believe that those things which he saith shall come to pass; HE SHALL HAVE WHATSOEVER HE SAITH.

— MARK 11:23

Let's examine what Jesus said in today's text: "*. . . and shall not doubt in his heart, but shall believe* [that is, believe in his heart] *that those things which he saith shall come to pass. . . .*" Those things that you *say* are your words — your confessions — and those words give you power over demons, disease, and circumstances.

What is it Jesus says you shall have? What you believe for? No. Many people think, *If I believe strongly enough, it will come to pass.* But at the same time, they are talking unbelief, so what they are asking for *cannot* come to pass!

Jesus did not say, "He shall have whatsoever he BELIEVETH"; He said, "*. . . he shall have whatsoever he SAITH.*"

For you do receive what you *say.* If you're not satisfied with what you have in life, then check up on what you are saying — what you are confessing. *All you have and all you are today is a result of what you believed and said yesterday!*

Confession: *I believe in my heart. I believe in my words.*

Words

Thou art snared with the words of thy mouth, thou art taken with the words of thy mouth.

— PROVERBS 6:2

Many Christians blame certain things on the devil, when actually they are taken captive by the words of their own mouths. One writer expressed it this way:

> You said you could not — and the moment you said it you were whipped. You said you did not have faith — and doubt arose up like a giant and bound you. You are imprisoned with your own words. You talked failure, and failure held you in bondage.

Our words dominate us. That's what Jesus was saying in Mark 11:23: "*. . . he shall have whatsoever he saith.*"

Never talk failure. Never talk defeat. Never acknowledge for one moment that God's ability or power cannot put you over. If you do talk failure or defeat, you are acknowledging that God cannot and has not put you over in life.

But thank God, He *can!* And He *has!* If you will believe right and talk right, you will walk in the reality of it!

Confession: *I refuse to talk failure. I refuse to talk defeat. God puts me over in life.*

What To Say

Ye are of God, little children, and have overcome them: because greater is he that is in you, than he that is in the world.
— 1 JOHN 4:4

What is the Holy Spirit doing in you?

Is the Holy Spirit just a "spiritual hitchhiker"? Does He just hitchhike a ride through life with you? Is He just some excess baggage for you to carry through life?

No! The Holy Spirit lives within you to help you!

He lives within you to strengthen you!

He lives within you to comfort you!

He lives within you to put you over in life!

Make positive confessions like this instead of talking failure and doubt.

Confession: *I believe that the Greater One lives in me. I believe that He is greater than the devil. I believe that He is greater than the tests and trials I may be facing. I believe that He is greater than the storm I may be going through. I believe that He is greater than the problems that may be confronting me. I believe that He is greater than the circumstances which may appear to have me bound. I believe that the Greater One is greater than sickness and disease. I believe that the Greater One is greater than anything and everything! And the Greater One dwells in me!*

Evil Report

... We be not able to go up against the people; for they are stronger than we. And they brought up an evil report of the land which they had searched unto the children of Israel, saying, The land, through which we have gone to search it, is a land that eateth up the inhabitants thereof; and all the people that we saw in it are men of a great stature ... giants ... and we were in our own sight as grasshoppers, and so we were in their sight.

— NUMBERS 13:31-33

Israel came out of Egypt and to the border of Canaan, to a place called Kadesh-barnea. From there they sent twelve men to spy out the land of Canaan. And the Bible says that ten of those spies brought back "an evil report."

What is an evil report? It is a report of doubt. (A believer has no more business peddling doubt than he does peddling dope!)

God had already told the children of Israel that He had given them this land flowing with milk and honey. They acknowleged that it was, indeed, a land flowing with milk and honey. "BUT," they complained, "there are giants in the land, and we are not able to take it!"

The children of Israel confessed what they believed. They *believed* they couldn't succeed. Then they *said,* "We can't." And they *received* exactly what they said! Israel accepted the majority report — the evil report — and said they couldn't take the land. And Israel got exactly what they said: God did not allow that generation to take the land.

Jesus said in Mark 11:23 that you will have whatever you say.

Confession: *I refuse to be a doubt peddler. I refuse to have an evil report!*

A Good Report

And Caleb stilled the people before Moses, and said, Let us go up at once, and possess it; for we are well able to overcome it.
— NUMBERS 13:30

And Joshua ... and Caleb ... spake unto all the company of the children of Israel, saying, The land, which we passed through to search it, is an exceeding good land. If the Lord delight in us, then he will bring us into this land, and give it us; a land which floweth with milk and honey. Only rebel not ye against the Lord, neither fear ye the people of the land; for they are bread for us: their defence is departed from them, and the Lord is with us: fear them not.
— NUMBERS 14:6-9

Joshua and Caleb were the two spies who had a good report. They didn't deny that giants were in Canaan; they simply added that the children of Israel would be able to overcome the giants.

"We are well able to overcome them," they said, "for the Lord is with us!" That was their good report.

Similarly, we believers must not stick our heads in the sand like ostriches and deny that problems and difficulties exist in our lives. Yes, the "giants" are there — but we are well able to overcome them, because the Lord is with us!

When you face the giants of life, don't have a negative confession. Don't talk doubt and have an evil report. *Faith always has a good report!*

Confession: *I am well able to overcome the giants in my life — because the Lord is with me! Greater is He who is in me than he who is in the world.*

Feelings

... for he hath said, I will never leave thee, nor forsake thee.
— HEBREWS 13:5

A woman came up to me at the close of a service where I had taught on faith. She was crying almost hysterically. She said, "Brother Hagin, pray for me!"

"What is the matter?" I asked.

"It seems like the Lord has forsaken me!"

"What awful sin have you committed to make the Lord forsake you?"

"As far as I know, I haven't done anything," she said. "It just seems like the presence of the Lord is gone from me."

"The Bible doesn't say we walk by 'seems like,' " I explained to her. "It says we walk by faith. And God's Word says that the Lord will never leave you, nor forsake you."

"I know that," she cried, "but it just seems like He has."

"You have more faith in 'seems like' than you have in the Bible."

"But I know what I feel!" she said, almost angrily.

"Yes," I said, "but I know my Jesus. Jesus said it, and I believe it. We cannot be concerned by what we feel."

If you start believing right, thinking right, and talking right, it won't be long until you'll be feeling right!

Confession: *Jesus will never leave me, nor forsake me. He said it. I believe it. And I say it.*

Praying and Saying

Therefore I say unto you, What things soever ye desire, when ye pray, believe that ye receive them, and ye shall have them. — MARK 11:24

Faith will work by *saying* without *praying* (notice Mark 11:23 doesn't mention praying), but faith also works by prayer.

However, when you *pray* it, you still have to *say* (or confess) it.

Let me repeat that: *Faith will work by SAYING it, or it will work by PRAYING it, but when you PRAY it, you still have to SAY it.*

Mark 11:23 and 24 brought me off a bed of sickness many years ago. After I had prayed, then I began to *say* (not think). I began to say out loud in my room, "I believe that I receive healing for my body." Then I specified each thing that was wrong with me: "I believe I receive healing for the heart condition. I believe I receive healing for the paralysis. I believe I receive healing for the incurable blood disease."

And just in case I had missed anything, I concluded, "I believe that I receive healing from the top of my head to the soles of my feet."

Within the hour every symptom of physical deficiency disappeared from my body, and I was standing on the floor beside the bed — healed!

Confession: *What things soever I desire, when I pray, I believe that I receive them. I confess what I believe. I hold fast to my confession. And I never fail to receive them.*

Believing First

Jesus said unto him, If thou canst believe, all things are possible to him that believeth.
— MARK 9:23

There is just a shade of difference in what you *believe* when you say it, and when you pray it.

Look again at Mark 11:23 and 24. Jesus didn't say, "Just believe." He told us exactly *what* to believe. Faith by saying is: "... *believe that those things which he saith shall come to pass ...*" (v. 23). When you believe that those things that you say shall come to pass, they haven't come to pass yet. But keep on believing that those things you said — be sure you've said it — shall come to pass. I always keep saying right in the face of contradictory circumstances, "It shall come to pass." What will happen then? "... *he shall have whatsoever he saith.*" Sooner or later you shall have it!

Faith by praying is: "... *when ye pray, believe that ye receive them ...*" (v. 24). *When* you pray. Not *after* you pray. Not next week. But *when* you pray — that very moment — believe. Believe what? Believe that you receive your requests. Begin to say, "I believe that I receive." And what will happen? "... *and ye shall have them*"!

Yes, the having will come, but the having doesn't come first. Believing comes first; then the having follows.

Confession: *I am a believer. When I pray, I believe that I receive. When I say, I believe that what I say shall come to pass.*

Faith for Finances

Let us hold fast the profession [confession] *of our faith without wavering; (for he is faithful that promised).*
— HEBREWS 10:23

When I've needed things in my own life, I've always stood on Mark 11:23 and said (or confessed) what I was believing God for. I've always just *said* it, and not *prayed* it.

(When another person is involved, however, what they believe can affect your prayers; especially if they are not in agreement with you.)

I haven't prayed about money for years, and I've never been without money. I always just say, "The money will come," and it comes. When I need a certain amount, I am specific in my confession: I specify the amount I need.

Once I needed $1500 by the first of the month. So I *said* it. And I kept saying it. During times of prayer, I didn't pray it; I just said, "By the first of the month I'll have $1500."

When the first of the month came, I had $1580, praise the Lord!

Confession: *I hold fast to my confession of faith without wavering. For He is faithful who promised. And I have what I say.*

In All Realms

Beloved, I wish above all things that thou mayest prosper and be in health, even as thy soul prospereth.

— 3 JOHN 2

The Lord Himself taught me about faith for finances many years ago. I was in the field ministry then, and I had been fasting and praying several days concerning a severe shortage of finances. The Lord spoke to me, saying, "Your trouble is you aren't practicing what you preach. You preach faith, but you don't practice it."

I protested, "Why, Lord, I do!"

"Oh, you practice faith when it comes to healing, and that is commendable," He said. "You've used your faith for salvation, the baptism in the Holy Spirit, and healing. But *faith is the same in every realm.* If you needed healing, you would claim it by faith and publicly announce you were healed. You must do the same thing for finances.

"I'll tell you what to do: First, never pray about money — that is, in the sense you have been praying. What you need is on earth. I'm not going to rain money down from heaven. It would be counterfeit, and I'm not a counterfeiter. What you need is down there. I made the earth and everything in it. And I didn't make it for the devil and his crowd. Claim whatever you need. Just say, 'Satan, take your hands off my money.' Because Satan is the one keeping it from you, not Me."

Confession: *Jesus has redeemed me from the hand of the enemy. And in the Name of Jesus, I have authority to claim what God has provided.*

Your Desires

Therefore I say unto you, What things soever ye desire, when ye pray, believe that ye receive them, and ye shall have them.
                                                    — MARK 11:24

"*What things soever ye desire....*"

No, not what things soever your grandpa desires. Not what things soever your aunt desires. Not what things soever your husband desires. Not what things soever your wife desires.

You *can* get your desires. However, if what you desire is not what someone else desires, you won't be able to push your desires off on them. Why? Because when somebody else is involved, their will comes into play on the situation.

Your faith will always work for you in your own life. And sometimes — not always — you can make your faith work for someone else.

Confession: *My faith always works for me in my own life. By divine wisdom I will know when I can make my faith work for others.*

Agreement

Again I say unto you, That if two of you shall agree on earth as touching any thing that they shall ask, it shall be done for them of my Father which is in heaven.

— MATTHEW 18:19

You won't be able to get somebody healed if you're believing that they will live, but they're believing they will die! There's no agreement there. When praying for others, it is important to get them to agree.

Usually, when someone comes to me with a prayer request, I say (if I can agree with it), "Let's join hands now and agree. Listen while I pray, and agree with my prayer. Because if we both pray at once and we don't pay attention to each other, you may be praying in one direction and I may be praying in another."

Once a woman came for prayer for a financial need. I prayed, "Father, we agree concerning the $100 this family needs by the first of next month. We agree that by the first of the month they'll have this extra $100. You said that if two of you agree as touching anything they ask, it shall be done. We agree that it is done, and we thank You for it now, in the Name of Jesus. Amen."

I looked at the woman and asked, "Is it done?" She started crying. "I hope it is," she said.

It wasn't. There was no agreement.

Confession: *If there are two of us . . . and we're on earth . . . and we agree as touching anything we ask in line with God's Word . . . it shall be done for us of our Father in heaven!*

Spiritual Babes

As newborn babes, desire the sincere milk of the word, that ye may grow thereby.
                                                    — 1 PETER 2:2

Under what circumstances can you help others?

As long as people are bona fide baby Christians, you can carry them on your faith and get things for them. It's the easiest thing in the world to get a new Christian healed. And it's comparatively easy to get Christians healed who have never been taught about divine healing. But God expects a little more from people who have had time and opportunity to know about spiritual matters.

When my wife and I were married in November 1938, she was Methodist, and she knew nothing about healing. In December, the first real Norther' blew into Texas and she got a sore throat. She said, "I'll have to go have my throat swabbed out. I'll have a bad throat all winter. I do every year."

That was a good opportunity to teach her about divine healing. Remembering Mark 11:23, I said, "No, we'll not have your throat swabbed out. This chronic sore throat will leave you and will never return."

It left. And all these years have come and gone, and she has never had a sore throat since. But I couldn't do that for her today, because she has developed her own faith, and God expects her to use it.

Confession: *I do desire the Word, that I may grow thereby . . . that my faith may grow thereby . . . so that I can help others.*

Faith for Another

For the eyes of the Lord run to and fro throughout the whole earth, to shew himself strong in the behalf of them whose heart is perfect toward him.

— 2 CHRONICLES 16:9

I was told I had an emergency telephone call. My sister, Oleta, was on the line, crying hysterically. She told me her daughter's baby had been born dead. The doctor now said the baby was alive, but he couldn't live, and he wouldn't be normal if he did live, because of a lack of oxygen to his brain. The doctor told the family, "The baby's face is deformed. It would be better if you didn't see him. We'll just dispose of the body when the baby does expire."

Oleta cried, "Benny [the baby's father] wants you to pray."

I knew my family were just babies when it came to spiritual matters, and I thought about Mark 11:23. "Oleta, where is Benny?" I asked.

"Right outside the phone booth," she replied.

"Now listen — the minute you hang up, turn to Benny and *say,* 'Benny, Uncle Ken said the baby will live and not die. He will be all right.' "

"Do you think so?"

"No, I don't *think* so; I *know* so. I've got Jesus' Word for it."

Not ten minutes later, a nurse came running out and told them, "You can see the baby! He's all right. While we were looking at him, his face filled out just like you'd blow up a balloon!"

You can't shut God out, if you'll believe Him.

Confession: *I believe God. I believe He desires to show Himself strong on my behalf.*

The Sent Word

He sent his word, and healed them....

— PSALM 107:20

An unsaved uncle of mine once contacted my mother. He wanted her to get in touch with me so I would pray for his daughter, who was dying. I told Momma when he called back to tell him that I said my cousin would live and not die.

"Oh, Son, have you heard from the Lord?" Momma asked. (She knew the Lord sometimes tells me things.)

"Yes, I've heard from the Lord. She will live and not die," I assured her.

"Praise the Lord. That's fine."

"Yes, I heard from the Lord in Mark 11:23."

"Oh," she said, her voice dropping in disappointment.

People put more emphasis on some kind of manifestation than they do the Word. Don't do that. Put the Word first.

When I told Momma again what to tell my uncle, she said, "Do you suppose it will work, Son?"

"Certainly it will work! Will the multiplication table work? No one ever says, 'I don't know if I've got enough faith to work the multiplication table.' If you'll work the multiplication table, it will work. And if you'll work Mark 11:23, it will work. It's the Word that does it. That's where some miss it. They think *they're* going to have to perform. No, *God* does it. All we're to do is what the Word tells us to do."

Confession: *God's Word works. I act on it, and it works for me.*

Growing Up

That we henceforth be no more children....
— EPHESIANS 4:14

I learned later that a few minutes after Momma told my uncle that I had said my cousin would recover, she suddenly opened her eyes and was perfectly all right! She was in Intensive Care, with three doctors around her bed, and the head surgeon had said she'd never come out of it.

I knew she would be well all the time, because Mark 11:23 said so. Through the years, I could make the Word work *once* with each of my relatives, bringing the supernatural to them. But I could never do it again. You see, that gave them concrete evidence that the Word worked. But when they'd come back to me the second time, I couldn't carry them any longer on my faith. God expected *them* to do a little bit the next time — at least to agree with me.

You can't always make the Word work for others. It is not right to carry people spiritually all their lives any more than it is for parents to carry their children in the natural all their lives. There comes a day when they have to get out on their own. And there comes a day when God says, "Put that big young'un down and let him walk!"

Confession: *I am growing up spiritually. I am growing in faith.*

Thanksgiving

Oh that men would praise the Lord for his goodness, and for his wonderful works to the children of men! And let them sacrifice the sacrifices of thanksgiving, and declare his works with rejoicing.

— PSALM 107:21,22

Our forefathers in the United States set aside a day each year to offer thanks to God for His blessings on them in this new world. He had blessed them both spiritually and materially.

We, too, should offer thanksgiving to God for the spiritual and material blessings of life He has bestowed upon us. And we should thank God for His loving protection and care for us.

This thanksgiving season, let's look into God's Word to see what He has to say about "the giving of thanks." We'll look into the New Testament, because we live under the New Covenant, to see what the New Covenant says we are to give thanks for.

Confession: *I praise the Lord for His goodness. I sacrifice the sacrifice of thanksgiving, and declare His works with rejoicing. I thank Him for the spiritual and material blessings of life. I thank God for His protection and care.*

First of All

I exhort therefore, that, first of all, supplications, prayers, intercessions, and giving of thanks, be made for all men; For kings, and for all that are in authority. . . .

— 1 TIMOTHY 2:1,2

When we follow the directions in God's Word and put first things first, we get results. This is especially true in regard to Scripture. If we follow the directions and put first things first, we can expect to receive from God the things He has provided for us.

"First of all" means first of all.

But also notice that along with supplications, along with prayers, along with intercessions, the Word inserts, "giving of thanks."

Lest we misunderstand exactly who he is talking about, Paul goes on to tell us exactly who these "all men" are. "Kings" would include presidents, rulers, and other leaders of nations. "All that are in authority" would include state, county, and city leaders, etc.

If we as Christians want to please God, who will we place as number one on our prayer and thanksgiving list? Ourselves? Our children? Our grandchildren? Our church? No. If we want to please God, we will have to do exactly as God said to do. We will have to pray and offer thanks *first of all* for all who are in authority.

Confession: *Thank You, Lord, for our president. Thank You for all who are in authority.*

Giving of Thanks

I exhort therefore, that, first of all, supplications, prayers, intercessions, and giving of thanks, be made for all men; For kings, and for all that are in authority....

— 1 TIMOTHY 2:1,2

The Word of God is clear on this subject. I believe many Christians have practiced this Scripture to some extent, but I believe we have somewhat neglected the "giving of thanks."

God wants us to offer thanksgiving to Him. And we have much to thank God for!

But too many Christians are always griping and talking about what is wrong with our nation. The Bible does not tell us as Christians to do that.

Instead, as Christians we are exhorted to make supplications, prayers, intercessions, and the giving of thanks for our leaders. (It is impossible that our prayers for them would work at the same time we're criticizing them.)

Confession: *I give thanks according to God's Word for my country's leaders. I give thanks for this great country.*

Purpose

... that we may lead a quiet and peaceable life in all godliness and honesty. For this is good and acceptable in the sight of God our Saviour; Who will have all men to be saved, and to come unto the knowledge of the truth.

— 1 TIMOTHY 2:2-4

God doesn't tell us to do something just to fill up space in the Bible. He has a purpose in mind. We are to pray for those in authority so that we who are Christians may lead a quiet and peaceable life. God is concerned about us, and He will work on our behalf, even when those in authority are not Christians.

God's ultimate purpose is that we be able to spread the Gospel freely. If we do not live under a stable government, the spreading of the Gospel is hindered. For example, times of political upheaval, war, travel restrictions, and other limitations hinder the spread of the Gospel. Jesus said, *"And this gospel of the kingdom shall be preached in all the world for a witness unto all nations; and then shall the end come"* (Matt. 24:14). The devil will try his best to see that this is not accomplished. Therefore, we are exhorted to offer intercessory prayer, supplications, and the giving of thanks for those who lead our nation.

Confession: *Father, I thank You for our leaders. I thank You because You hear and answer prayer, and because You are working on our behalf.*

Thank You, Father

Giving thanks unto the Father, which hath made us meet to be partakers of the inheritance of the saints in light: Who hath delivered us from the power of darkness, and hath translated us into the kingdom of his dear Son: In whom we have redemption through his blood, even the forgiveness of sins.

— COLOSSIANS 1:12-14

The New Covenant tells us we should be giving thanks unto the Father because He has made us able to be partakers of something. Of what? "*. . . of the inheritance of the saints in light*"!

The Amplified Bible translates verse thirteen as, "[The Father] has delivered and drawn us to Himself out of the control and the dominion of darkness. . . ."

God Himself has delivered us from the control of Satan! Satan's kingdom is the kingdom of darkness. God's kingdom is the kingdom of light. The Father has made us able to be partakers of the inheritance of the saints in light. He has delivered us out from under the control and dominion of darkness. Satan has no control over us. He cannot dominate us.

And we are told to thank God for that!

Confession: *Thank You, Father, for making me fit to be a partaker of the inheritance of the saints in light. Thank You for delivering me out of the authority of darkness. Thank You for transferring me into the kingdom of your dear Son — the kingdom of light.*

Changing of Lords

For sin shall not have dominion over you: for ye are not under the law, but under grace. — ROMANS 6:14

Another translation of today's text reads, "For sin shall not lord it over you."

Sin and Satan are synonymous terms. Therefore, we could read this verse, "For Satan shall not have dominion over you," or, "Satan shall not lord it over you."

The reason why Satan cannot lord it over you is found in Colossians 1:13: The Father has delivered you out from under Satan's control and dominion.

The moment you were born again and became a new creature in Christ Jesus, Jesus became your Lord. Now He is the one who dominates you; Satan is no longer your lord. Satan can no longer lord it over you. When you were born again, Satan's dominion over you ended — and Jesus' dominion over you began!

And anything that is of Satan — sickness, disease, bad habits, or whatever — can no longer lord it over you!

Confession: *Jesus is my Lord. Thank You, Father. Thank You for delivering me from the power of Satan. Thank You because Satan can no longer lord it over me. Thank You because sickness, disease, and bad habits can no longer lord it over me. Thank You because Satan has no dominion over me!*

A Great Plan

Christ hath redeemed us from the curse of the law, being made a curse for us: for it is written, Cursed is every one that hangeth on a tree.

— GALATIANS 3:13

Part of the inheritance which Colossians 1:12-14 tells us we should be giving thanks to the Father for, is "... *redemption through his blood*" (v. 14).

What are we redeemed from? From the curse of the law. And what *is* the curse of the law? The only way to find out, is to go to the law and see what it says the curse is.

The term "the law," as found in the New Testament, refers to the first five books of the Bible, the Pentateuch. Reading there, we find that the curse, or punishment, for breaking God's law is threefold:

1. Spiritual death (Gen. 2:17)
2. Poverty (Deut. 28:15-68)
3. Sickness (Deut. 28:15-68)

Galatians 3:13 tells us that Christ has redeemed us from the curse of the law, and Colossians 1:12-14 tells us to thank God for it! We are to thank the Father for this great plan of redemption which He planned and sent the Lord Jesus Christ to consummate!

Confession: *Thank You, Father, for your great plan of redemption which You planned and sent the Lord Jesus Christ to consummate! Thank You because I am redeemed from death! Thank You because I am redeemed from poverty! Thank You because I am redeemed from sickness! Thank You, Father!*

Spirit Filled

And be not drunk with wine, wherein is excess; but be filled with the Spirit; Speaking to yourselves in psalms and hymns and spiritual songs, singing and making melody in your heart to the Lord; Giving thanks always for all things unto God and the Father in the name of our Lord Jesus Christ.
— EPHESIANS 5:18-20

"I just can't thank God like I should," some people have said.

You can if you follow Paul's admonition in Acts 19:1-6 "... *be filled with the Spirit.* ..." And just after giving this admonition to these Pentecostal people, Paul gives some ways to keep filled with the Spirit: *"Speaking to yourselves in psalms and hymns and spiritual songs, singing and making melody in your heart to the Lord.* ..." An overflowing heart will be your testimony! Your cup will be full and running over! You will have a song in your heart!

"Giving thanks always for all things. ..." Your heart is thankful. You give thanks for all of God's blessings. You even can give thanks for every test. You don't give thanks for what the devil has done, but you give thanks for the Word, for the opportunity to see God at work, and for the fact that you know God can make all things work together for your good.

Confession: *I keep being filled with the Holy Spirit. I speak in the Spirit. I sing in the Spirit. I make melody in my heart to the Lord. And I am thankful.*

Giving Thanks Well

Let the word of Christ dwell in you richly in all wisdom; teaching and admonishing one another in psalms and hymns and spiritual songs, singing with grace in your hearts to the Lord. And whatsoever ye do in word or deed, do all in the name of the Lord Jesus, giving thanks to God and the Father by him.

— COLOSSIANS 3:16,17

In every thing give thanks: for this is the will of God in Christ Jesus concerning you.

— 1 THESSALONIANS 5:18

Notice how yesterday's Scripture and today's Scripture are very similar.

A song in the heart and the giving of thanks simply go hand in hand.

And if you are filled with the Holy Spirit, you will experience this praise and this thanksgiving.

If you don't, then you're simply not filled with the Spirit. Be filled! (*See* John 7:37-39; 14:16-17; Acts 1:4-5; 2:4; 8:14-17; 10:44-46; 19:1-3,6.) Then you'll have a spirit of praise and a spirit of thanksgiving.

Confession: *I let the word of Christ dwell in me richly. I benefit from teaching and admonishing in psalms and hymns and spiritual songs. I sing with grace in my heart to the Lord. Whatever I do in word or deed, I do in the Name of the Lord Jesus. I give thanks to God the Father by Him.*

Be Filled

For he that speaketh in an unknown tongue speaketh not unto men, but unto God: for no man understandeth him; howbeit in the spirit he speaketh mysteries. . . . For if I pray in an unknown tongue, my spirit prayeth, but my understanding is unfruitful. What is it then? I will pray with the spirit, and I will pray with the understanding also: I will sing with the spirit, and I will sing with the understanding also. Else when thou shalt bless with the spirit, how shall he that occupieth the room of the unlearned say Amen at thy giving of thanks, seeing he understandeth not what thou sayest? For thou verily givest thanks well, but the other is not edified. — 1 CORINTHIANS 14:2,14-17*

God has given to the Church a divine, supernatural means of communication with Himself! God is a Spirit. When we speak in tongues, our spirit is in direct contact with God, who is a Spirit! We are talking to Him by a divine, supernatural means. By this means we can ". . . *bless with the spirit.* . . ." And we can ". . . *give thanks well.* . . ."

When Paul referred to "he that occupieth the room of the unlearned," he meant those persons who are unlearned in spiritual things. If you invited me to dinner and said, "Please give thanks," and I prayed in tongues, you wouldn't know what I had said. You wouldn't be edified. Therefore, Paul said it would be better to pray with the understanding in that instance.

But notice that the Word of God declares that praying in tongues is a perfect way to give thanks well!

Confession: *I shall bless God with the Spirit. I shall give thanks well.*

Midnight Praise

And at midnight Paul and Silas prayed, and sang praises unto God: and the prisoners heard them.

— ACTS 16:25

Singing and praising and thanksgiving all go together.

Paul and Silas had been beaten with many stripes, cast into prison, and their feet put in stocks. But at midnight they prayed and sang praises to God — aloud. The other prisoners heard them!

Most people in similar circumstances would have griped and complained. If they had been like some modern Christians, Silas would have said, "Paul, are you still there?" And Paul would have answered, "Where else would I be?"

Silas would have complained, "I'll tell you, my poor back is hurting so bad. I don't understand why God sent this on us. I don't understand why God let this happen to us. He knows we've tried to serve Him and do our best!"

That kind of praying would have gotten Paul and Silas further in — instead of out! God didn't have them thrown in jail; the devil did. But there's truth and instruction here to help us in our midnight hour — the hour of test, of trial — when the storms of life come. That's the time to pray, praise, sing, and give thanks to God!

Confession: *I praise and thank God at all times. I never have a "poor old me" attitude. I keep an attitude of praise at all times.*

Worship

As they ministered to the Lord, and fasted, the Holy Ghost said. . . .
— ACTS 13:2

This is the prayer of worship — ministering to the Lord.

It is true that God is concerned about us. He is interested in us, and wants to meet our needs, because He has told us to ask. But my personal observation is that too large a percentage of our praying is, "Give me, give me, give me."

We need to take time in our individual prayer lives, in our gatherings, in our churches, to wait on God and to minister to the Lord. In this kind of atmosphere God can move. As they ministered to the Lord and fasted, the Holy Spirit manifested Himself!

God made man for His own pleasure so He would have someone with whom to fellowship. He is our Father. We are born of God. No earthly parent ever enjoyed the fellowship of his children more than God enjoys the fellowship of His sons and daughters.

Take time to minister to the Lord: To pray. To wait on God. To tell Him how much you love Him. To praise Him. To thank Him for His goodness and mercy.

Confession: *Make up your own confession. Practice today's lesson by ministering to the Lord.*